Invisible
WEAPONS

The Science of Biological and Chemical Warfare

HEADLINE SCIENCE ··· Biological and Chemical Warfare

Biological and Chemical Warfare ···

by Don Nardo

Content Adviser:
Debra Carlson, PhD, Department of Biology,
Normandale Community College, Bloomington, Minnesota

Science Adviser:
Terrence E. Young Jr., MEd, MLS,
Jefferson Parish (Louisiana) Public School System

Reading Adviser:
Rosemary G. Palmer, PhD, Department of Literacy,
College of Education, Boise State University

Compass Point Books • 151 Good Counsel Drive, P.O. Box 669 • Mankato, MN 56002-0669

This book was manufactured with paper containing
at least 10 percent post-consumer waste.

Library of Congress Cataloging-in-Publication Data
Nardo, Don, 1947–
Invisible weapons : the science of biological and chemical warfare / by Don Nardo.
    p. cm.—(Headline Science)
Includes bibliographical references and index.
ISBN 978-0-7565-4217-7 (library binding)
1. Biological warfare—Juvenile literature. 2. Biological weapons—Juvenile literature. 3. Chemical warfare—
Juvenile literature. 4. Chemical weapons—Juvenile literature.
I. Title. II. Series.
UG447.8.N298 2010
358'.3—dc22   2010005231

Editor: Anthony Wacholtz
Designer: Ashlee Suker
Media Researcher: Eric Gohl
Production Specialist: Jane Klenk

Photographs ©: DVIC/Sgt. Kevin R. Reed, USMC, cover (bottom); Shutterstock/mike_expert, cover (inset, left), 34;
Shutterstock/Dmitry Chernobrov, cover (inset, middle), 5; DVIC/MC1 Bobbie G. Attaway, cover (inset, right), 37;
Library of Congress, 7; DVIC/NARA, 9, 10; Getty Images Inc./AFP/Roberto Schmidt, 11; Getty Images Inc./Time Life
Pictures/Brian Seed, 13; Getty Images Inc./MPI, 14; CDC/Margaret Parsons, Dr. Karl F. Meyer, 15; CDC/Jean Roy, 17;
AP Images/Lawrence Livermore National Laboratory, 18; Shutterstock/Carolina K. Smith, M.D., 19; Getty Images
Inc./The Frank S. Errigo Archive, 21; Getty Images Inc./Popperfoto, 22; AP Images/Chuck Robinson, 23; AP Images,
24; Getty Images Inc./Remi Benali, 26; AP Images/U.S. Army-Pine Bluff Arsenal, 27; Getty Images Inc./Tim Matsui,
29; Getty Images Inc./AFP, 30, 40; Getty Images Inc./AFP/Asahi Shimbun, 31; AP Images/Dario Lopez-Mills, 33;
Getty Images Inc./Time Life Pictures/Chuck Nacke, 35; AP Images/Douglas C. Pizac, 38; AP Images/Wong Maye-E,
41; Getty Images Inc./Joe Raedle, 42; United States Mission Geneva, 43.

Visit Compass Point Books on the Internet at *www.capstonepub.com*

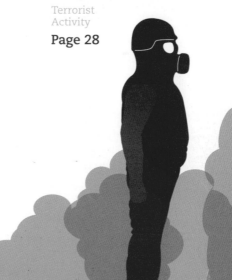

OBAMA ADMINISTRATION TAKES A NEW APPROACH TO BIOLOGICAL WEAPONS

The New York Times, Mark Landler
December 8, 2009

The Obama administration plans to announce a new policy [to] curb the spread of biological weapons [that] will focus on increasing health security to reduce the impact of outbreaks of infectious disease, whether natural or man-made, administration officials said. ...

The major hurdle ... is that biological weapons are simply harder to monitor than chemical or nuclear weapons. They can be produced in small labs, using equipment readily converted from peaceful uses, by a rapidly growing and mostly private biotechnology industry.

The Obama administration recognized the importance of addressing the concern over bioterrorism. People across the world were horrified to learn of several chemical and biological attacks over the last few decades. In the 1980s Iraqi dictator Saddam Hussein unleashed poison gas on his own people, killing thousands. In 2001 authorities believe an American scientist tried to murder U.S. government officials using deadly anthrax spores. The threat of biological and chemical warfare continues today.

Biological weapons, which use diseases to harm or kill people or other living things, have hit the news often in recent years. So have chemical weapons, which use the poisonous

Infantry in the Russian army practiced various ways to contain outbreaks at a chemical warfare training session in 2009.

KEEPING CURRENT

News changes every minute, and readers need access to the latest information to keep current. Here are a few key search terms to help you locate up-to-the-minute biological and chemical warfare headlines:

agroterrorism

chemical agents CDC

Atlantic Storm smallpox

chemical warfare

bioterror NOVA

FEMA terrorism

biowarfare

weapons stockpiles

properties of certain natural chemical substances to do the same. Both chemical poisons and the disease carriers that make up biological weapons are frequently called agents.

Chemical and biological weapons are classified as weapons of mass destruction (WMD). This term refers to their potential destructive powers. If used in a crowded area, chemical and biological weapons can kill hundreds or even thousands of people. Nuclear weapons are also WMD.

CHEMICAL WEAPONS IN THE PAST

About 70 types of chemical agents have been developed for use in warfare. Most of the agents were made in the 20th century, but a few were created much earlier. In fact, evidence shows that chemical warfare existed in Africa during the Stone Age. Archaeologists have found arrowheads there that were once coated with the venom of snakes and scorpions.

Another example of early chemical warfare comes from ancient Greece. In the fifth century B.C., the Spartans used smoke from burning sulfur against their enemies. A similar chemical agent was used in China in the following century. Soldiers dug tunnels while attacking cities, and the defenders directed smoke from burning mustard plants into the tunnels.

During the American Civil War (1861–1865), New York schoolteacher John Doughty proposed using chlorine gas as a weapon. He suggested putting liquid chlorine in a cannon. He said that when the shell exploded, the liquid would be changed into a gas. Then the gas would be released into the enemy ranks. As it turned out, no such toxic shells were used in the war.

Fifty years later chemical weapons were used—with horrible effects. During World War I (1914–1918), 124,000 tons (112,490 metric tons) of chemical agents

During World War I, gas masks became standard equipment for U.S. soldiers fighting overseas.

were produced. They included chlorine gas, phosgene gas, and mustard gas. About 51,000 tons (46,266 metric tons) of these toxic materials were used on European battlefields. They killed 85,000 people and injured more than 1.1 million. In the 1930s the Japanese used chemical weapons against the Chinese. In the 1980s Iraq's president, Saddam Hussein, used several kinds of poison gas on both his Iranian enemies and his own citizens.

MAIN CHEMICAL WEAPONS AGENTS

Scientists divide chemical weapons into groups. Each group has certain characteristics that set it apart. Some affect the nervous system, while others blister the skin or cause choking.

The horrible effects of choking agents were documented during World War I. An expert described a German chlorine gas attack on French and Algerian soldiers:

CHEMICAL WEAPONS AGENTS

Each group of chemical weapons agents is designed to produce a certain effect. Prolonged exposure to many of the chemical agents may lead to death.

Group	Types	Symptoms
nerve agents	sarin, tabun, VX, cyclosarin, soman, some insecticides	blurred vision, headaches, nausea, vomiting, suffocation, seizures
blood agents	cyanogen chloride, hydrogen cyanide	cherry-red skin color, confusion, nausea, vomiting, difficulty breathing, seizures
blister agents (vesicants)	mustard gases	skin blisters, severe skin and eye irritation, lung damage
choking agents (pulmonary agents)	chlorine, phosgene, hydrogen chloride	sore throat, coughing, wheezing, chest pains, lung damage

As the wall of yellow-green mist approached their lines, the French and Algerian troops smelled a pungent [bitter] odor that tickled their throats … and filled their mouths with a metallic taste. Moments later, the … toxic cloud swept over them, veiling the world in greenish murk as if they had suddenly been plunged several feet underwater. … The chlorine seared their eyes and burned the lining of their bronchial tubes, causing … coughing, violent nausea, [and] a stabbing pain in the chest. Hundreds of soldiers collapsed in agony, their silver badges and buckles instantly tarnished greenish black by the corrosive gas.

DELIVERY OF CHEMICAL AGENTS

The Germans unleashed the deadly chlorine gas by a method called dispersion. They placed containers of

Allied soldiers with gas masks marched through a poisonous gas cloud in France during World War I. Soldiers without masks quickly felt the effects of the dangerous chemicals.

the chemical agent on the battlefield, opened them, and allowed the gas to spread and drift across enemy lines. This method was unreliable because its success depended on weather conditions, which could change rapidly. If the wind changed direction, the lethal gas could float back to their own troops.

A more efficient method to deliver chemical agents was devised later and is still used today. Agents are put

During World War I, containers of chlorine gas were spread out in a line over several miles. Wind carried thick clouds of the gas across enemy lines.

< SEEKING WMD IN IRAQ >

In 2002 the U.S. government claimed that Iraqi dictator Saddam Hussein had chemical and biological weapons. There was a widespread fear that he would use the weapons against his neighbors or the United States. In 2003 the United States led an invasion of Iraq to drive Hussein from power. However, no weapons of mass destruction were found there. Many people still worry that terrorist organizations will get their hands on chemical and biological weapons.

U.S. soldiers in chemical protection suits searched a potential site for WMD in Iraq.

inside containers—such as bombs, shells, missiles, and warheads. Then they are shot or dropped through the air. When the containers explode, they release the toxic gases. The gases can also be delivered by large sprayers like those used to spray insecticides. The gases can be released by hand or remote control.

The effectiveness of the delivery systems depends on the users. Individuals and groups with little money or expertise tend to use simpler, less reliable systems. Weapons programs run by national governments usually have the money and knowledge needed to create more complex and effective delivery systems.

MAILMAN TO DELIVER AID IN CASE OF ANTHRAX ATTACK

>>> Associated Press
December 30, 2009

If the nation ever faces a large-scale attack by a biological weapon like anthrax, the U.S. Postal Service will be in charge of delivering whatever drugs and other medical aid Americans would need to survive. In an executive order ... President Barack Obama put the Postal Service in charge of dispensing "medical countermeasures" to biological weapons because of its "capacity for rapid residential delivery."

Under the new order, federal agencies must develop a response plan that includes possible law enforcement escorts for Postal Service workers and gives anthrax "primary threat consideration."

Biological weapons, also called bio-weapons, use harmful microbes or microorganisms. Nonscientists often call them germs, so the use of biological weapons is often called germ warfare. Some viruses and microbes are harmless or even beneficial to people. Others cause diseases that have ravaged humanity for thousands of years. It is the harmful viruses and microbes that bioweapons makers try to harness. The process of using them in weapons is known as weaponizing.

BIOWEAPONS IN THE PAST

Weaponizing viruses and microbes is nothing new. People waged biological warfare in ancient, medieval, and early modern times. Only one major difference separates early bioweapons from modern ones. Early bioweapons makers did not know about the existence of germs. The germ theory of dis-ease was not introduced until the 1800s. They did not understand how or why the weapons worked, but they could see that some diseases spread through physical contact. That was enough to encourage them to create simple but effective biowarfare methods.

Bomb shells have been specifically made for biowarfare. The shells would break in half when dropped, releasing germ-carrying insects.

It was not unusual, for example, to use diseased corpses of animals and humans as weapons. The most common tactic was to put the corpses in wells or streams to contaminate the enemy's drinking water. During sieges attackers sometimes used catapults to throw diseased corpses into forts and cities to infect the inhabitants. A well-known example of this took place in 1347. A warlike Asian people, the Mongols, besieged the Italian colony of Kaffa, on the northern coast of the Black Sea. The attackers hurled dead bodies of bubonic plague victims into the city. So many people caught the disease that Kaffa had to surrender.

Another deadly disease, smallpox, was used as a weapon in colonial America. In 1763 Fort Pitt (in what is now Pennsyl-vania) was attacked by Native Americans of the Shawnee and Delaware tribes. During a truce negotiation, the fort's British commander gave Indian messengers some blankets. The messengers did not know that the blankets had recently been used by smallpox victims. Since the Indians

Indian tribes confronted British officers after discovering they had been given blankets contaminated with smallpox during earlier peace talks.

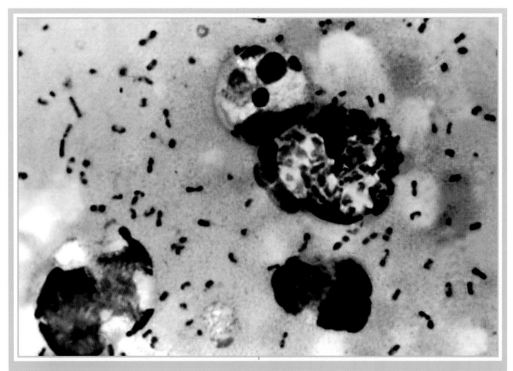

Traces of the Yersinia pestis *bacteria from a patient revealed the presence of the bubonic plague.*

HEADLINE SCIENCE

had never been exposed to the disease, their immune systems could not resist the virus. How many Indians died as a result is not known for certain.

MODERN PLAGUE AND SMALLPOX THREATS

Today bubonic plague and smallpox are still two of the main biological agents used by bioweapons makers.

Bubonic plague, often just called the plague, has killed millions of people over the centuries. Once plague bacteria enter a person's body, they travel to the lymph nodes, which are part of the immune system. There they multiply and form egg-shaped lumps, often in the underarms or groin. After a few days, the bacteria move to the lungs and other vital organs. The victim can bleed from the skin and even die if the disease is untreated. Fortunately, it can be treated with antibiotics when caught in its early stages.

A challenge for people intent on using plague as a weapon is getting the bacteria. They have to come from a living thing. One way is to capture an animal infected with the disease. Plague is common among prairie dogs, squirrels, rats, and mice in the southwestern United States. Plague bacteria can be removed from a sample of infected tissue. The bacteria can then be grown in large numbers in glass containers in a lab.

Another challenge for someone planning to use plague as a weapon is delivering the disease to a human population. According to biologists and other experts, the most effective method is an aerosol spray. After growing the bacteria in a lab, the weapons maker dries the bacteria into a powder and places the powder in an aerosol container. Someone can then take the container to a crowded part of a city and begin spraying. Because the powdered bacteria are microscopic, they are undetectable, and the victims would be unaware of the danger. They would breathe in the spray and not realize they were infected until days later.

Experts warn that smallpox is a disease that could be weaponized in a spray container. The classic symptoms of smallpox include fever, chills, and outbreaks of pus-filled sores. The death rate among the millions of people who have gotten the disease over the centuries has been high. Smallpox has killed

NOW YOU KNOW

Among the many biological agents used in making bioweapons is the bacterium that causes Q-Fever. One of the most contagious bacteria, it infects both animals and humans when they breathe tiny particles of it floating in the air. Experts say it is rarely fatal, but those who contract it can become very sick.

After a person has been exposed to the smallpox virus, it takes between seven and 17 days for the symptoms to appear.

defeat the virus. Their effort was successful. In October 1977 the last known case of smallpox was reported in Africa. But scientists kept samples of the disease in labs for research purposes. Some people worry that the samples might be stolen and made into bioweapons. However, these samples are well-guarded.

ANTHRAX AND OTHER BIOLOGICAL AGENTS

Besides plague and smallpox, most bioweapons experts have focused on about 12 other biological agents, including anthrax. A disease of cattle, sheep, and other livestock, anthrax spreads through spores (small seed-like capsules). The spores lie in the soil until a grazing animal swallows them. Once inside the creature's body, the spores change into active bacteria, which infect the host.

20 percent to 60 percent of adults and 80 percent of children with the disease.

In the late 1960s, medical experts from many countries set out to

Humans can be infected with anthrax too. The spores can enter the body through an open cut on the skin. A person might also breathe them into the lungs. Most of those who inhale the spores will die if they are not treated. If caught within two or three days, anthrax can be cured with antibiotics. Because breathing in the spores can be deadly, the main delivery method is to get the spores into the air. Experts say this can be done by spraying them from a container. The spores can also be dropped from an airplane or placed in a bomb or other explosive device.

In a simulation of an anthrax attack, a yellow cloud is superimposed over an aerial photograph of Seattle, Washington, to show the widespread area that would be affected.

Such an easy delivery method has made anthrax a frequent choice of bioweapons makers. But several other agents also have been used. One causes botulism, a dangerous medical condition usually caused by eating spoiled meat. The toxin is so deadly that even a microscopic amount is enough to kill a person. The victim usually dies of lung failure.

Agents such as anthrax appeal to bioweapons makers for several reasons. First, they cost much less than many other weapons, such as machine guns and tanks. Second, small amounts can cause a lot of damage. Also, such agents can continue to infect people over time. In addition, bioweapons can be easily delivered by missiles, sprays, or food products. Finally, large amounts of them can be made in just a few days. For these reasons, biological weapons remain a threat to human communities.

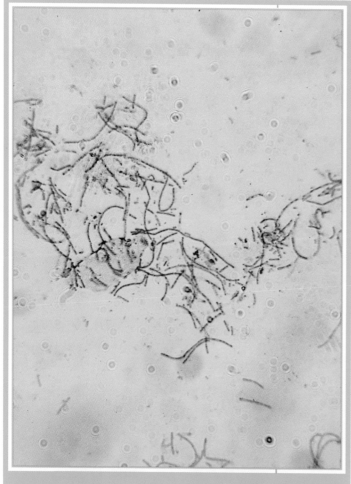

Microscopic view of Bacillus anthracis, *the bacteria found in anthrax*

LA PORT ADDS SHIP TO SCREEN FOR BIOLOGICAL WEAPONS

>>> Associated Press
February 10, 2010

A new ship to detect chemical and biological weapons has been launched to protect the ports of Los Angeles and Long Beach.

The Los Angeles Sheriff's Department said Wednesday it started using the $3 million vessel this week. It is staffed by explosives experts and equipped with tools to screen cargo ships for threats before they enter the nation's busiest port complex.

The experts board the ships and screen for substances used for weapons of mass destruction. Deputies have also added a helicopter to screen for radioactive material, while the ship's sonar system looks for underwater threats.

Advances in science in the 20th century allowed several countries to develop chemical and biological weapons. Efforts by nations to collect large amounts of these weapons happen through state-sponsored weapons programs. Weapons produced by the programs were used during World War I, World War II, the Vietnam War, and at other times during the 1900s.

Also during the 20th century, individuals, countries, and international groups condemned state-sponsored chemical and biological weapons programs. Use of these weapons was called inhumane and unethical. Several international treaties banned their use.

During World War II, U.S. soldiers performed training exercises involving chemical and biological warfare. The soldiers wore gas masks during the exercise, while a dog carrying a first aid kit was fitted with a special muzzle that acted as a filter.

But experts warn that some countries, such as Iran, probably still have programs for developing chemical and biological weapons. Other nations, they say, may no longer have active programs, but they may have stockpiles of weapons. The danger exists for two reasons: The stockpiles can be secretly sold to nations that sponsor terrorism, refuse to honor international treaties, or otherwise threaten global peace. They also can be sold to terrorist groups.

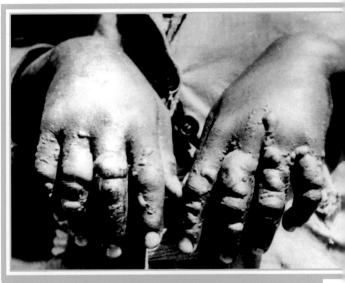

Soldiers in the early 1900s were not prepared for the effects of mustard gas. Their uncovered hands quickly blistered after exposure to the gas.

CREATION OF DEADLY STOCKPILES

Among the first nations to develop stockpiles of chemical and biological weapons in the 1900s were France and Germany. Both created and used chemical weapons, including mustard gas, during World War I. Evidence shows that the Germans also created and used bioweapons in the war. They developed anthrax spores in labs. Then they infected horses with the spores and let them loose in France. The exact number of French animals and people that caught the disease is unknown.

In the years after the war, several other countries—including Britain—began chemical and biological weapons programs. Britain may have used chemical weapons on people in the Middle East, parts of which it then controlled. Italy used mustard gas during its invasion of Ethiopia in the 1930s, killing or injuring 15,000 people.

Meanwhile, the Soviet Union started its own chemical and biological weapons programs. Soviet researchers developed stockpiles of bubonic plague bacteria.

The United States was not far behind in creating similar programs. In the 1940s alone, the U.S. government spent more than $40 million developing bioweapons. Extensive research was done at a bioweapons

NOW YOU KNOW

In 1941 Soviet bioweapons scientists infected prisoners of war with bubonic plague. Some of the prisoners escaped and passed the infection on to the residents of several Mongolian villages. At least 4,000 people died.

Stockpiles of the deadly VX nerve agent were held in a secure building in Indiana while the military developed methods to destroy it. The building was surrounded by razor wire and protected by armed guards.

factory in Vigo, Indiana, during World War II, but none of the weapons it designed were used

After the war the United States continued research into chemical and biological weapons. Large amounts of nerve agents had been developed by the 1960s. Several biological agents, including those that cause anthrax and tularemia (rabbit fever), were created.

EFFORTS TO STOP WEAPONS PRODUCTION

Even while the Americans, British, and others were developing and stockpiling chemical and biological weapons, they were also trying to limit their use. The first major attempt was the Geneva Protocol. Although several nations signed the treaty in 1925, it did little to halt the buildup of chemical and

After World War II, German soldiers worked to dismantle and dispose of bombs that carried mustard gas and other toxic agents.

biological weapons. This was largely because it banned only the *use* of these deadly weapons. The document said nothing about weapons production or storage. In addition, there was no mention of allowing international inspections of weapons plants.

As time went on, therefore, stockpiles of these weapons continued to grow. In response, some people and groups around the world became increasingly concerned. The United States finally took drastic action. In 1969 President Richard Nixon ended all production of U.S. chemical and biological weapons. He also ordered that all of the country's stockpiles be destroyed.

Soon afterward the leaders of several nations called for new rules to strengthen the Geneva Protocol. In 1972 almost 90 countries signed the Biological Weapons Convention (BWC). It banned both the use and production of biological weapons. It also said that stockpiles of bioweapons should be destroyed. A similar treaty regarding chemical weapons, the Chemical Weapons Convention (CWC), was signed in 1993. It said in part:

> Each State Party to this Convention undertakes never under any circumstances: ... To develop, produce, otherwise acquire, stockpile or retain chemical weapons, or transfer, directly or indirectly, chemical weapons to anyone; [or] to use chemical weapons. ... Each State

< THE SUBWAY EXPERIMENT >

American bioweapons makers have conducted tests in public places without telling anyone what was happening. In 1966, for example, the "Subway Experiment" took place. A bacterium known as BG was placed in a New York City subway. It was thought to be harmless. The intent was to see whether a biological agent released in a single subway station could spread throughout the tunnel system. The results showed that it did exactly that. More than a million people were exposed to the bacterium, though none experienced any ill effects.

Party undertakes to destroy chemical weapons it owns or possesses, or that are located in any place under its jurisdiction or control.

Almost every nation on Earth signed the CWC. As of 2010 the only countries that had not signed were Angola, the Democratic People's Republic of Korea, Egypt, Somalia, and Syria. Several countries, including France, China, and the United States, still had chemical weapons facilities. Following the CWC rules, they openly declared the facilities. They also indicated how the weapons would be destroyed or converted to other uses.

Workers at the Tooele Army Depot in Utah wore pressurized suits while transporting biological and chemical agents to an incinerator.

Workers placed a container of M-55 rockets loaded with sarin gas into an incinerator at the Pine Bluff Arsenal compound in White Hall, Arkansas. Almost 4,000 tons (3,628 metric tons) of chemical weapons were destroyed at the Arkansas compound.

CHANCE OF ATTACKS

Some experts say the BWC and CWC have made the use of the weapons less likely. They also have claimed that the risk of attacks is lower for another reason: a fear of reprisal. In other words, the strong possibility that the target country would strike back with its own WMD may be enough to discourage a would-be attacker. This situation, however, mainly applies to nations with large populations at risk. Terrorist groups have much less to lose. That means they are much more likely to use chemical and biological weapons.

CHAPTER 4: Terrorist Activity

WMD REPORT-U.S. REMAINS 'DANGEROUSLY VULNERABLE'

USA Today
September 9, 2008

The United States remains "dangerously vulnerable" to chemical, biological and nuclear attacks seven years after the 9/11 attacks, a forthcoming independent study concludes. ... The group [that made the study] includes leaders of the disbanded 9/11 Commission ... that investigated government missteps before the 2001 terror attacks on the United States.

"The threat of a new, major terrorist attack on the United States is still very real," says the report. ... "A nuclear, chemical or biological weapon in the hands of terrorists remains the single greatest threat to our nation. ... While progress has been made in securing these weapons and materials, we are still dangerously vulnerable."

Several studies on WMD and terrorist groups have been conducted by experts and government officials in recent years. All agree that small, independent terrorist groups are more likely to use chemical and biological weapons than nations are.

The deadly weapons appeal to terrorists for several reasons. First, they are effective but cost little. Tanks, missiles, attack helicopters, and other advanced weapons of war are extremely expensive. On the other hand, chemical and biological weapons are cheap and easy to make. With only "a few thousand dollars," two terrorism experts say, a terrorist can produce enough chemicals and germs

A Hazardous Materials Response Team in Seattle, Washington, carefully examined a mailbox where a vial containing an unknown substance was discovered.

In 2007 a truck filled with chlorine exploded upon impact near a police station in Ramadi, Iraq. The explosion, which was set off by TNT in the truck, killed 27 people.

to "kill thousands of people."

Terrorists also favor the weapons because they are easy to use. Both chemical and biological agents can be released simply by spraying them in crowded areas. This exposes many people to the dangerous materials. Because the sprays are invisible, victims are at first unaware that they have been targeted. The terrorists have enough time to get far away before anyone knows an attack has occurred.

Terrorists know that their chances of being caught and punished are low. It is often hard for law enforcement officials to tell who used such weapons. Finding and capturing the culprits months or years after an attack is almost impossible.

RECENT CHEMICAL AND BIOLOGICAL ATTACKS

Attacks in recent years have shown how easy it is to make and deliver chemical and biological weapons. Members of the terrorist organization Al-Qaida unleashed chlorine gas on Iraqi citizens in 2007. More than 350 people became ill, and some were in serious condition.

The most famous recent terrorist chemical attack took place in March 1995. It was carried out by members of a Japanese cult known as Aum Shinrikyo. Cult members believed that their god wanted them to destroy humanity. They released sarin nerve gas in the subway system of Japan's biggest city, Tokyo. Twelve people died, and more than 5,000 were injured.

The Aum Shinrikyo cultists did not limit themselves

to chemical weapons. A few years earlier, they had tried to make a bioweapon. First they created large quantities of botulinum toxin, an extremely lethal poison made from

Passengers waited to receive medical attention after inhaling sarin gas that was released into the subway system in Japan.

bacteria. Then they weaponized the toxin by putting it in spray containers. Finally, they released the spray into the air in downtown Tokyo. However, the terrorists had not made the poison concentrated enough, so no one died.

Anthrax spores were released in the United States in 2001. The main targets were the editors of a newspaper, the *New York Post*, NBC News anchorman Tom Brokaw, and U.S. Senators Tom Daschle and Patrick Leahy. Their offices each received an envelope containing spores. None of the intended targets was hurt. But

at least 23 other people came down with anthrax. They were infected by spores that leaked out of the envelopes before reaching their destination. Five of those who contracted the disease died.

The incidents occurred soon after the September 11, 2001, terrorist attacks in New York City and Washington, D.C., so many people suspected the anthrax had been unleashed by Muslim extremists. Not until 2008 did authorities find evidence of the contrary. The suspected terrorist was an American scientist, Bruce E. Ivins, who worked in an Army lab. He committed suicide before he was formally charged.

THE THREAT OF AGROTERRORISM

Direct chemical or biological attacks on people are not the only way that terrorists might use WMD. They might also attack a nation's crops and livestock. Such assaults on food supplies are called agroterrorism. Although chemical agents can be used, very

NOW YOU KNOW

Besides releasing poison gas in Tokyo's subway system, the Japanese cult Aum Shinrikyo targeted Japan's national legislature, the emperor's palace, and the U.S. Navy base at Yokosuka. All of the assaults failed.

Postal workers in São Paulo, Brazil, wore protective masks while sorting mail to prevent the potential threat of inhaling anthrax.

large amounts would be needed to destroy thousands of fields and animals. Experts point out that biological agents are more practical because much smaller amounts can do a lot of damage.

Agroterrorism might appeal to terrorists for reasons of morality. In the past some terrorists—such as the 9/11 hijackers—were willing to com-

mit mass murder. However, some use terrorist acts mainly to make a political statement. They may be reluctant to kill large numbers of people. These terrorists, experts say, may be more likely to destroy crops and livestock to make their statement.

A successful agroterrorist attack on the United States would certainly make a powerful statement. It could

A bioterrorist attack on the nation's crops would have devastating effects on the economy. The crops affected by the attack would have to be destroyed. The attack might also scare consumers from buying the crops in the future.

also be disastrous for the country. The danger is not just that some people might die or become ill from eating tainted food. The economic consequences would be equally devastating, if not more so. A 2005 editorial in *The Christian Science Monitor* warned:

With agriculture making up 13 percent of the economy and 18 percent of employment, the devastating results of an agroterror attack could go far beyond human casualties and include an economic crisis and a loss of confidence in government. Even a false alarm over agroterrorism can prove costly. Some may recall the

Chapter 4: *Terrorist Activity*

1989 Chilean grape scare: A terror group phoned the U.S. embassy in Chile claiming cyanide was in that country's grapes. The cost was an entire crop of Chilean fruit and about $200 million in lost revenue.

The United States has a much larger population and is a much larger food producer than Chile. So a terrorist attack on the U.S. food supply could have major consequences. According to some experts on agroterrorism, the country might suffer tens of billions of dollars in losses. That would make many kinds of food harder to get and more expensive. The potential threat of such an incident shows that terrorists have a variety of ways to use WMD. Experts say that is ample reason for setting up defensive measures to counter such attacks.

Chilean grocers were forced to remove fruit from their shelves in 1989 after two tainted grapes were discovered.

U.S. CALLED UNREADY TO COUNTER MAJOR BIOLOGICAL ATTACK

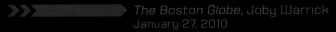

The Boston Globe, Joby Warrick
January 27, 2010

More than eight years after the deadly 2001 anthrax attacks, the United States is still unprepared to respond to a major biological terror attack, a congressionally appointed commission said yesterday. ...

The report ... gave the White House and Congress "F" grades, saying they have failed to build a rapid-response capability for dealing with bioterror threats or provide adequate oversight over security and intelligence agencies.

The bipartisan panel cited the government's uneven response to the swine flu epidemic as evidence of a lack of preparedness for a large-scale crisis.

Members of the commission looked into whether the country is properly prepared to deal with a major biological attack. They decided that the United States is not well enough prepared for such an attack. Their conclusion came as a surprise to many people working in the government on both the national and state levels. Many defensive measures against biological and chemical weapons have been put in place in the United States since September 11, 2001. However, the commission members felt that there was still work to do.

In the case of biowarfare, for example, the federal government has

Firefighters demonstrated the process of decontamination during a biowarfare drill in South Korea in 2009.

A microbiologist at the Life Sciences Test Facility in Utah worked with sarin, anthrax, and other deadly agents in an airtight laboratory.

outlined emergency medical plans to combat disease outbreaks. Many states and cities have staged special drills to deal with an outbreak. First responders, including firefighters, police, doctors, and nurses, have reacted to simulated attacks. The hope is that this will better prepare them for the real thing if it does occur. Most experts agree that these and other measures have increased the nation's ability to respond to a biological or chemical attack.

Yet the 2010 commission's report made it clear that much more needs to be done. The commission's members pointed out that more money is needed for equipping and training first responders. Strengthening U.S. defenses against chemical and biological threats, they say, must be an ongoing effort.

BETTER PREPAREDNESS

The effort continues to be made on the national, state, and local levels. The need for better preparedness on the national level was shown in 2005. American and foreign government officials took part in a drill involving a simulated biological attack under the code name Atlantic Storm. Former U.S. Secretary of State Madeleine Albright played the part of the U.S. president. Officials from several nations played world leaders who were meeting with her in Washington, D.C.

In the midst of the conference, as part of the drill, the participants received news of a terrorist attack. Al-Qaida, the group behind the 9/11 disasters, had released smallpox virus in the United States and a few other nations. The pretend leaders tried to respond to the mock emergency. Each set his or her country's national terrorism response plans in motion, but it wasn't enough. A study of the staged crisis showed that the spread of smallpox could not have been contained by the proposed plans of action. Within six months, millions of people worldwide would have died, and large sectors of the global economy would have collapsed. The exercise clearly troubled the participants. One later said he was shocked at "how little prepared many countries were."

On a smaller scale, communities must also be ready to respond to chemical or biological attacks. Experts point out that local preparation for a chemical attack involves several key factors. One is having special equipment in place to detect the presence of chemical agents. There must be a reliable alarm system to notify first responders and the public. And the first responders must have quick access to protective equipment, if needed. Such equipment includes

Police officers in biohazard suits helped people posing as gas attack victims during a nuclear, biological, and chemical weapons exercise in Osaka, Japan.

gas masks and chemical-resistant suits. Finally, they must have supplies of substances designed to counteract dangerous chemical agents.

Local preparations for biological attacks include making sure that medical personnel are trained to recognize the diseases that might be unleashed. Special teams of doctors and nurses need to be ready to respond within minutes. Medical authorities say it is equally important to stockpile sufficient quantities of vaccines. Having enough vaccines is crucial in stopping the spread of any diseases introduced in an attack.

PREVENTING ATTACKS

Some experts have suggested another way to combat the threat of chemical and biological weapons: prevent their use in the first place. The 1972 Biological Weapons Convention and the 1993 Chemical Weapons Convention have dramatically slowed the production of such weapons. Yet some countries may still be making them in secret. Both the BWC and CWC lack the power to require that the weapons be destroyed and the offender nations be punished.

To address this problem, an addition to the BWC and CWC called a protocol was proposed in 2001. The

Members of the Chemical, Biological, Radiological, and Explosive Unit in Singapore demonstrated how to inspect a potential WMD container.

protocol would let weapons inspectors investigate suspected weapons programs across the globe. Any nation caught cheating on the treaties would be subject to international pressure to end such programs. But the United States did not sign the new protocol. The reason given by officials in President George W. Bush's administration was that it might expose important U.S. military secrets and threaten national security.

The idea of identifying potential attacks and defending against them is a policy that remains in place under the Obama administration. However, the administration added measures designed to prevent the attacks from happening in the first place. This includes closer studies of disease

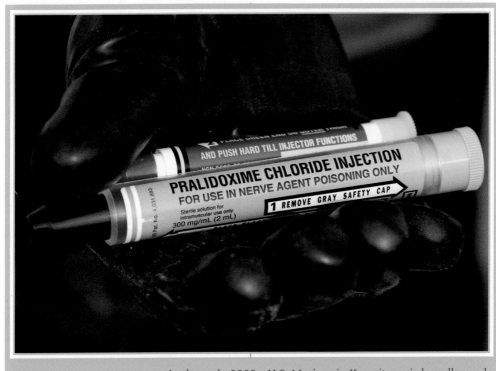

In the early 2000s, U.S. Marines in Kuwait carried needles and pralidoxime, an anti-nerve gas agent, in case of a chemical attack.

In December 2009 Ellen Tauscher, the under secretary for Arms Control and National Security, presented a new strategy for preventing biowarfare to the Biological Weapons Convention in Geneva, Switzerland.

epidemics worldwide and monitoring terrorist activity. The policy also calls for international cooperation in an effort to identify potential bioterrorists and to find ways to keep them from developing bioweapons.

Other ways of preventing chemical and biological attacks have been proposed. One is to destroy all surviving samples of smallpox virus. This would keep the virus from falling into the hands of terrorists or rogue nations. In addition, experts call for police, the FBI, and other law enforcement agencies to work together more effectively. These and other measures may reduce the likelihood of chemical and biological warfare and make the world a safer place.

1347
The Mongols catapult bodies of bubonic plague victims into an enemy city, spreading the disease

1763
A British officer gives blankets carrying smallpox virus to some American Indians, infecting them

1914–1918
The French and Germans use poison gas during World War I

1925
Many nations sign the Geneva Protocol, which calls for bans on chemical and biological weapons

1930s
Italian soldiers use mustard gas during their invasion of Ethiopia

1966
As an experiment, U.S. weapons makers release harmless biological agents in New York City's subway system

1969
U.S. President Richard Nixon stops the nation's chemical and biological warfare programs

1972
The Biological Weapons Convention, which bans germ warfare, is signed by most countries

1980s
Iraqi dictator Saddam Hussein uses poison gas against his Iranian enemies and his own people

1993
Most nations sign the Chemical Weapons Convention, banning use of such weapons

1995
Members of a Japanese cult, Aum Shinrikyo, release poison gas in Tokyo's subway system

2003
The United States invades Iraq, in part to keep Saddam Hussein from using chemical and biological weapons

2007
Members of Al-Qaida in Iraq use chlorine gas against Iraqi citizens

2009
An American scientist warns that terrorists may be planning to release disease-carrying insects in the United States and other countries

2010
The Obama administration puts emphasis on biowarfare prevention in addition to identifying and defending against attacks

Timeline

GLOSSARY

agroterrorism
terrorist attacks on a nation's or city's
food supply

anthrax
disease spread by spores that usually
affects livestock

antibiotic
medicine that fights infections caused
by microorganisms

biological weapons
weapons that use viruses and
microorganisms to spread diseases
through human populations

chemical weapons
weapons that use chemical
substances to kill or harm people
or other living things

first responders
police officers, firefighters, doctors, or
other professionals who are first on the
scene in a disaster

microorganisms (microbes)
microscopic organisms

nerve agents
poisonous substances, such as sarin gas,
that impair the nervous system

phosgene
gas used as a choking agent on World
War I battlefields

protocol
treaty or an individual section of a treaty

pulmonary agents
poisonous substances, such as chlorine,
that cause people or animals to choke

spores
tiny, seedlike capsules that are part
of the life cycles of some organisms,
including those that cause anthrax

toxic
poisonous

vesicants
blister agents

virus
nonliving, microscopic particle that can
cause disease

weaponize
to make something into a weapon

WMD
weapons of mass destruction,
including chemical, biological,
and nuclear weapons

FURTHER RESOURCES

ON THE WEB

FactHound offers a safe, fun way to find Internet sites related to this book. All of the sites on FactHound have been researched by our staff.

Here's all you do:

Visit *www.facthound.com*

FactHound will fetch the best sites for you!

FURTHER READING

Baker, David. *Biological, Nuclear, and Chemical Weapons: Fighting Terrorism.* Vero Beach, Fla.: Rourke, 2006.

Harmon, David E. *Chemical and Biological Weapons: Agents of War and Terror.* New York: Rosen, 2009.

Phillips, Tracey A. *Weapons of Mass Destruction: The Threat of Chemical, Biological, and Nuclear Weapons.* Berkeley Heights, N.J.: Enslow, 2007.

Rudy, Lisa Jo. *Bioterror: Deadly Invisible Weapons.* New York: Franklin Watts, 2007.

LOOK FOR OTHER BOOKS IN THIS SERIES:

Altering the Biological Blueprint: The Science of Genetic Engineering

Cure Quest: The Science of Stem Cell Research

Goodbye, Gasoline: The Science of Fuel Cells

Feel the G's: The Science of Gravity and G-Forces

Invisible Exposure: The Science of Ultraviolet Rays

Outbreak!: The Science of Pandemics

Performance-Enhancing Risks: The Science of Steroids

Recipe for Disaster: The Science of Foodborne Illness

SOURCE NOTES

Chapter 1: Mark Landler. "Obama Administration Takes a New Approach to Biological Weapons." *The New York Times*. 8 Dec. 2009. 10 March 2010. www.nytimes.com/2009/12/09/world/09biowar.html

Chapter 2: "Mailman to Deliver Aid in Case of Anthrax Attack." Associated Press. 30 Dec. 2009. 10 March 2010. www.msnbc.msn.com/id/34636216

Chapter 3: "LA Port Adds Ship to Screen for Biological Weapons." Associated Press. 10 Feb. 2010. 10 March 2010. http://hosted.ap.org/dynamic/stories/U/US_PORT_SECURITY?SITE=AP&SECTION=HOME&TEMPLATE=DEFAULT&CTIME=2010-02-10-15-39-57

Chapter 4: "WMD Report: U.S. Remains 'Dangerously Vulnerable.'" *USA Today*. 9 Sept. 2008. 10 March 2010. www.usatoday.com/news/washington/2008-09-09-wmd-report_N.htm

Chapter 5: Joby Warrick. "U.S. Called Unready to Counter Major Biological Attack." *The Boston Globe*. 27 Jan. 2010. 10 March 2010. www.boston.com/news/health/articles/2010/01/27/us_ill_prepared_for_biological_attack_panel_finds/

ABOUT THE AUTHOR

In addition to his numerous acclaimed volumes on ancient civilizations, historian Don Nardo has published several studies of modern scientific discoveries and phenomena. Don lives with his wife, Christine, in Massachusetts.

INDEX